the

ONE
HABIT

The Ultimate Guide to
Increasing Engagement and
Building Highly-Effective Teams

Cover Illustration Copyright © 2017 by Elena A. Newton
Designed and typeset by Elena A. Newton in 12/16 Minion Pro

ISBN 978-0-692-90099-4
First Edition First Printing

Xmetryx Press
an Imprint of Xmetryx, LLC
Scottsdale, AZ USA
www.xmetryx.com
press@xmetryx.com

For the exceptional team leaders who contributed to this Guide, and who continue to elevate the experience of their people—you, and your winning teams, are the future of work and organizations.

Table of Contents

The ONE Habit

Introduction

The Architecture of Highly-Effective Teams

This whole game of business
revolves around one thing.
You build the best team, you win.

—*Jack Welch*
Former CEO of GE

Jack Welch led one of the most dramatic corporate turnaround and growth stories of the late 20th century. Welch estimated that he spent nearly a third of his time focused on developing leaders and the leadership team at GE.

During his tenure as the head of GE (one of the largest industrial conglomerates in the world) the company created more wealth for its investors than any company ever in the recorded history of U.S. publicly traded companies. GE's value increased 4000% from 1981 to 2001.

Teams are shaping the future of work and organizations. In response, companies invest upward of $160 billion each year on leader training and development; yet, most of those programs fail to turn ideas into habits that lead to more effective, higher-performing teams.

*What distinguishes exceptional teams
and team leaders from the rest?*

Exceptional team leaders have mastered the one habit of consistently closing experience-expectation gaps across key relationships. Those key relationships, and the motivations and emotions that drive them, are at the heart of an architecture used by the most highly-effective teams. This architecture reflects what exceptional team leaders actually do to build and sustain energized, engaged teams. It begins with solid team fundamentals, supported by the universal drivers of individual motivation and engagement at work. At the core of this architecture is *the ONE Habit*.

This guide gives you a clear framework, with tools and actions, to put in place the Architecture of Highly-Effective Teams™, and to develop *the one habit* that consistently leads to superior team performance.

The Architecture of Highly-Effective Teams

The first chapter of this guide, *Team Fundamentals*, helps you lay the groundwork for your team architecture. We've provided you with clear steps and examples to build the solid foundation of a highly-effective team.

In the next chapter we explore the second layer in the architecture, individual motivation at work, and how it impacts team performance. We uncover the elements of motivation that every team leader needs to know and understand, and we connect them to the core of highly-effective teams — key relationships.

The third chapter of this guide demonstrates the importance of key relationships and how they impact team performance. You'll learn why gaps between what people expect and what they experience in these key relationships affects their motivation, engagement, and performance.

In *Measuring Gaps* we introduce you to Xmetryx — a set of web-based software tools designed to develop the one habit by measuring, understanding, and tracking gaps across those key relationships. This gives you the insights to close the gaps and build the one habit that is at the heart of engaged, highly-effective teams.

The fifth chapter, *Closing Gaps*, describes the actions exceptional team leaders take to nurture the key relationships that define the employee experience, and build and maintain high-performance teams. We describe how you can use Xmetryx to increase the people's energy, improve their engagement, and deliver team excellence.

Getting Started summarizes the steps, tools, and information you need to build the best team. We've extracted the essence of the earlier chapters, and included a checklist to ensure you've covered all the key points.

Use the templates and examples in *Resources* for generating ideas. For more information on the fundamentals of team building, motivation, key relationships, and the experience expectation dynamic, check the Additional Reading section of that chapter.

Within this Guide, we've embedded layers of information. Look for each of the <u>red underlined</u> terms in the *Glossary* to get deeper insights about their importance in the Architecture of Highly-Effective Teams and their effect on *the one habit*.

The Ultimate Guide

We don't take the description *the Ultimate Guide* lightly. This Guide is designed for team leaders who aspire to excellence and are driven to build exceptional teams. Developed by team leaders for team leaders, it contains the essence of years of experience and research into the practices that lead to team excellence. This guide gives you a clear framework, with tools and actions, to put in place the Architecture of Highly-Effective Teams, and to develop *the one habit* that consistently leads to superior team performance.

We are what we repeatedly do.
Excellence, then, is not an act,
but a habit.

—*Aristotle, 384–322 BCE*

Team Fundamentals

The Foundation of Highly-Effective Teams

What does it take to build and sustain an energized, highly-effective team? In addition to discipline, patience, and perseverance, the Architecture of Highly-Effective Teams starts with the team fundamentals of:

- Purpose
- People
- Support

These fundamentals are easy to identify, yet can be tough to execute—there are no short-cuts to getting it right. Just like building a new house, the time you put into getting a solid foundation right at the start will save you time and trouble down the road. The remainder of this chapter gives you clear steps for putting these solid team fundamentals in place. You can find examples and templates for these fundamentals in the *Resources* chapter at the end of this Guide.

The 1st Fundamental: Purpose

The first fundamental of building highly-effective teams is the development of a clear and compelling team purpose that aligns with the goals of the broader organization, along with specific performance measures.

Develop a compelling team purpose
and set clear performance goals

Developing a clear and compelling team purpose can be done on a white board, in a relatively short amount of time, by working through the following steps with your team:

1. Goals. Develop a set of team specific goals and performance measures that align with the broader unit or organization goals.

2. Relationships. Identify the key relationships, as well as the formal and informal communications processes, needed to accomplish the team goals.

3. Context. Describe the context in which the team will operate. For example, is this a global virtual team, a co-located project team, or a permanent functional team.

4. Competencies. List the key competencies the team members must have to be successful delivering the team goals given the context and relationships. Identify any gaps / areas to strengthen. These will be further addressed in the 3rd *Fundamental.*

5. Purpose. Reflecting on the team goals, relationships, context, and competencies, develop a one to two-sentence team purpose statement. Make sure that it is clear and compelling, and specific to the team.

Notes: Team Goals and Purpose

_____

_____

_____

_____

_____

_____

_____

_____

_____

_____

_____

_____

_____

_____

_____

_____

_____

The 2nd Fundamental: People

The second fundamental of highly-effective teams focuses on the people who make up your team. Building energized, engaged teams means balancing between the needs of the individuals and the manner in which they cooperate and collaborate as a team.

The first, and most important, step is to establish healthy *team norms* — and to ensure that all the members of your team actively embrace these norms. Team norms are the traditions, behavioral standards, and unwritten rules of your group. As a team leader, be purposeful in building a team that incorporates the norms of emotional / social intelligence, psychological safety (everyone should feel that they can take risks sharing a range of ideas), and conversation equality.

Next, be sure that there is a clear, concise role for every team member. Good *job design* should describe the purpose of the role, and consider the *role content* and *role context*. The role context should take into account the reality of the organizational culture, the team norms, everyday work processes, the nature of key relationships and dependencies, as well as key measures of success.

Last, determine the **optimal team size** to accomplish the team's goals. By focusing on the goals, you can ensure you don't over-scope or under-scope the project relative to the number of people needed to be successful. Typically, effective teams range from 4 to 7 people, and team effectiveness begins to break down once a team exceeds 12 people.

Notes: Norms, Job Design, Team Size

_____

_____

_____

_____

_____

_____

_____

_____

_____

_____

_____

_____

_____

_____

_____

_____

_____

The 3rd Fundamental: Support

The third fundamental of highly-effective teams is ensuring team members receive the optimal level of support in terms of resources, information, and training.

Resources should be sufficient for each member of your team to achieve the goals developed in the *1st Fundamental*. To do this, start by developing a Resources Map:

1. List each goal or team objective.

2. Match that against the resources needed to accomplish the goals.

3. Identify any gaps between the current resources and what is needed.

4. Identify an owner and a target date for closing the gap.

Information must flow freely, not only among your team members, but also across teams (such as within the relationships defined in the *1st Fundamental*). It is equally important to identify what information is needed to accomplish the team's objectives, along with the source of that information (another team, training, etc.).

In a process similar to developing a Resources Map, develop a Key Information Map with your team. Map your team's goals to their information needs, and identify any gaps, along with owners and target dates for closing those gaps.

Training. There should be a straightforward path for team members to develop new skills and competencies that will benefit the team as well as the team member's career (step 4 in the *1ˢᵗ Fundamental*). Develop a clear plan for every team member to build on their strengths and hone new skills. If the team members do not all directly report to you, then the Training and Development Plan should be drawn up in cooperation with the direct manager.

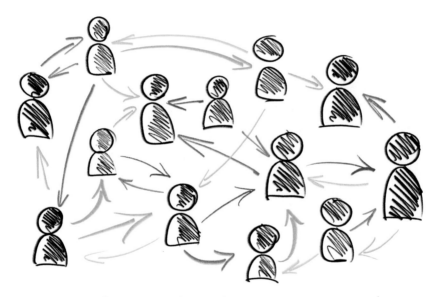

Ensure information flows freely among team members and across teams. Also, provide the resources and training your group needs to be successful.

Notes: Resources, Information, Training

_____

_____

_____

_____

_____

_____

_____

_____

_____

_____

_____

_____

_____

_____

_____

_____

_____

_____

_____

Foundation of the Architecture

Purpose, *people*, and *support*. Those are the essential foundational building blocks of a highly-effective team. They sound easy, yet few organizations ensure that they are in place before sending a team off to accomplish their goals. Successfully building on that foundation requires the next level in the architecture: a working knowledge of what motivates the individuals on your team.

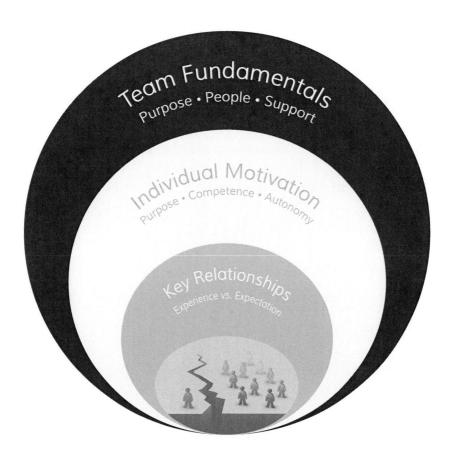

Notes from the Field

The Situation

Years of rapid growth, and an intense focus on quarterly sales, led to one business unit of a global IT company neglecting their existing customers. The result was slower sales and lower margins.

The Mission

Balance the focus of short term sales with an equally strong focus on customer success, to improve existing customer sales and profitability.

The Plan

Restructure the business unit, creating cross-functional teams responsible for customer success. Give each customer success team leader responsibility for building a focused, effective team.

The Outcome

The business unit leadership team undertook a rigorous restructuring and change management process. Team leaders were carefully selected and customer success teams established. Despite these efforts, nearly a year later there was no measurable improvement in the customer experience.

Analysis & Observations

Conversations with the customer success team leaders, team members, and the business unit managers revealed two gaps in the team fundamentals:

1. A lack of clear job design

2. A lack of team-leader training

While the teams' purpose was clear, the team leaders' job design (their purpose in the context of the business unit structure and goals) were not. This, combined with failing to invest in developing team leadership skills, resulted in a misalignment of the teams' goals with the business unit goals, underperformance versus expectations, and a poor experience for the team leader and team.

Those gaps resulted in the team leaders defaulting to old, comfortable habits and behaviors rather than pushing themselves and their teams to develop the competencies needed to accomplish the mission.

If your actions inspire others to dream more, learn more, do more, and become more, you are a leader.

—*John Quincy Adams*
6th President of the United States of America

Motivation at Work

What Drives
Individuals and Teams

What is Motivation?

By nature, people are oriented toward taking action to achieve specific outcomes. These outcomes may range from goals driven by basic needs, such as food and shelter, to more intrinsic — even subconscious — needs such as the drive to find meaning and purpose in one's work or life. *Motivation is energy that is directed by our thoughts and feelings.* When applied to the world of work, the phenomenon of motivation helps us understand what drives individuals and teams.

Broadly, motivation can be divided into two overlapping domains: intrinsic, which focuses on motivation that comes from within, and extrinsic which consists of external, contextual influences.

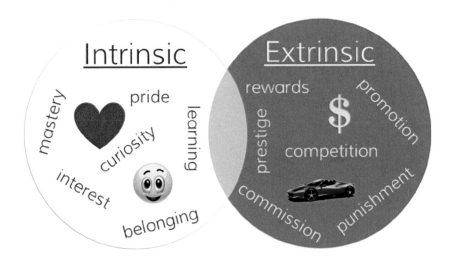

Motivation can be divided into two overlapping domains: intrinsic (internal) and extrinsic (external).

Intrinsic motivation involves engaging in an activity because it is inherently interesting, compelling, and satisfying. Whether it is a small joy like reading a novel, carving a perfect turn in fresh powder, or taking a new idea and "putting a dent in the universe", actions that are fueled by intrinsic motivation are, by far, the most powerful.

Extrinsic, contextual influences are important to consider, but are often controlled outside the scope of team leaders and teams. The exception is when they become part of the more powerful intrinsic motivators. For example, if a team leader encourages skill mastery, it may originally be an extrinsic motivator, but can be internalized by team members and eventually become intrinsic to them.

People's interest in, and engagement with, the work they do plays a key role in energy and motivation. That motivation is fueled by three basic, universal psychological needs: _purpose_, _autonomy_, and _competence_.

Finding meaning and purpose in our work is at the heart of positive energy and motivation. Exceptional team leaders ensure that there is clarity in how each team member's work contributes to the purpose and goals of the team, the broader organization, and the aspirations of the individual.

In addition, team leaders must ensure that team members have the freedom to determine how to deliver results. This autonomy is essential to keeping talented people energized and engaged.

Finally, great team leaders understand the relationship between competencies, confidence, and results. They continuously invest in developing the capabilities that lead to their team having confidence in their ability to win.

Purpose
Having a sense of belonging and that one's work makes a difference

Autonomy
Having some control over one's own role and priorities

Competence
Developing and demonstrating one's capabilities and capacities

Notes: Purpose, Autonomy, Competence

_____

_____

_____

_____

_____

_____

_____

_____

_____

_____

_____

_____

_____

_____

_____

_____

_____

_____

Motivation at Work

The core psychological needs of _purpose_, _autonomy_, and _competence_ are universal and cross-cultural. Fulfillment of those needs is fundamental to fueling motivation at work, and driving individual and team energy, engagement, and performance.

Those basic needs of purpose, autonomy, and competence are fulfilled (or not) through _key relationships_ such as those with team leaders, supervisors, and coworkers.

Any gaps between people's experiences and expectations in those key relationships affect the motivation and energy of the entire team.

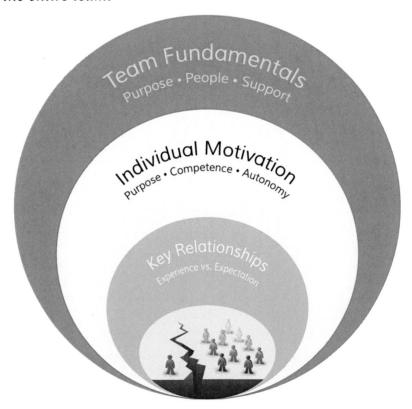

The Science Behind Motivation at Work

From the turn of the 19th century through the decade following World War II, motivational drive theories (behavioral and psychodynamic) played a prominent role in Western experimental and applied psychologies. The advent of cognitive motivation theories precipitated the decline of the motivational drive construct.

During the latter part of the 20th century and the early part of the 21st century, motivational theories returned to the mainstream, fostered by frameworks built around evolved and acquired human needs, and intrinsic motivation. Within the context of this revival emerged the macro-theory of motivation that was developed by Edward Deci and Richard Ryan (1985): Self-determination Theory (SDT).

Within the SDT framework, people derive high motivation levels from connections with others, resulting in a commitment to a target outcome (Battistelli, Galletta, Portoghese, & Vandenberghe, 2013). Over time, SDT researchers consistently showed that engaged, motivated individuals experienced improved physical and psychological well-being (Ryan & Deci, 2000).

Notes from the Field

The Situation

An established software company excelled at supporting its large customer base, but faced slowing growth due to a lack of product innovation. Organizational silos inhibited the flow of information from customers to coders, and an engineering team culture focused on maintenance vs. generating new ideas stifled innovation.

The Mission

To define, design, and develop a next generation cloud-based product within 12 months.

The Plan

Break down organizational silos, introduce new rapid development tools and techniques, and drive a customer centric design approach by appointing the head of Global Services as the team leader for the project.

The Outcome

With strong support from the CEO, the team leader established a clear compelling purpose for the team, assembled a mix of internal and external talent, and gave them the freedom to execute. The team delivered breakthrough product ahead of schedule and under budget.

Analysis & Observation

By ensuring that she had solid team fundamentals (purpose, people, and support) in place the team leader laid the foundation for a successful project. By focusing on the key motivational drivers across her team members, the result was an energized, engaged, effort with outstanding results.

The learnings and practices from this project also prepared the organization for broader cultural change and a shift toward rapid innovation.

In its essence, engagement is a function of the strength of important relationships.

—*Jeb Hurley*
Author, The ONE Habit

Key Relationships

The Heart of Highly-Effective Teams

Experience vs. Expectation

Recall a great day at work. What made it great? For most people the answer is simple: feedback from a client or customer that you and your team "made a difference"; an opportunity to demonstrate your knowledge and skills; or being part of an energized team.

Next, recall a bad day at work. What made it a bad day? Again, the answers are typically simple: a manager or team leader that micro-manages; uncooperative peers; or a lack of peer and manager support to accomplish your goals.

What is common across both the great and not-so-great days is that it was your key relationships that made the difference. More specifically, it was your expectation of that key relationship, versus your actual experience.

Now, think about an important relationship in your life: your spouse or significant other, your boss or your coworkers.

Consider the expectations you have of that person or those people.

Reflect on how you feel about your actual experience in the relationship.

Notes: Experience vs. Expectation

_____

_____

_____

_____

_____

_____

_____

_____

_____

_____

_____

_____

_____

_____

_____

_____

_____

_____

_____

_____

If your experience meets or exceeds your expectations, how does it make you feel? How does it affect the level of energy and engagement you express in the relationship?

If there is a large or growing gap between your experience and your expectations, how does it affect your energy and your level of engagement?

It is our experiences versus our expectations, in the context of key relationships, that affects the direction of those relationships: are we engaged or disengaged; is our relationship developing or deteriorating.

- *Expectations* form the baseline of how we judge and respond to experiences. They are personal and individual, and based on past experiences or the experiences of others.
- *Experiences* drive our feelings and behavior.

The experience-expectation dynamic is broad and deep, and is built upon four pillars of behavioral science research: Engagement Theory, Self-Determination Theory, Psychological Contract Theory, Expectancy Disconfirmation Theory. Read about these key theories in the *Glossary*.

Gaps between our experiences and our expectations affect motivation, energy, and engagement. *Measuring, understanding, and closing experience-expectation gaps across key relationships is essential to building and sustaining energized, highly-effective teams.*

Mastering the Architecture of Highly-Effective teams begins with putting in place solid team fundamentals, applying a working knowledge of individual and team motivation, and consistently closing experience-expectation gaps across key relationships. Specifically, across key work relationships such as those between the team leader and team members, among team members of the same team, and between teams in an organization that depend on collaboration to accomplish goals.

The one habit of consistently closing experience-expectation gaps begins with measuring and understanding those gaps, then taking specific actions based on that information. How you do that is the subject of the following chapters.

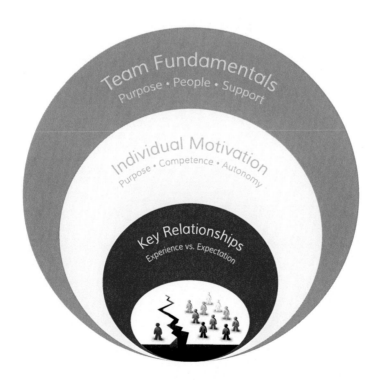

There is no greater challenge than to have someone relying upon you; no greater satisfaction than to vindicate his expectation.

—*Kingman Brewster*
Former President of Yale University
and US Ambassador to England

Measuring Gaps

Across Key
Relationships

Introducing Xmetryx

Organizational success is increasingly dependent upon the effectiveness of teams and their leaders. One of the most powerful predictors of team and team leader performance is the health of the key relationships between team members and their leader, with their team mates, and with other teams (both as individuals and as a whole) whose support is needed to accomplish their goals. Measuring and tracking team member experiences versus the expectations they have of those relationships is critical to building highly-effective teams. *The critical question is how?*

This chapter introduces Xmetryx, a set of software tools designed to help team leaders build the one habit of closing experience-expectation gaps. Xmetryx (derived from experience metrics) gathers insights by measuring gaps between experiences and expectations, maps the results so you can take action against those insights, and tracks the progress of efforts to close gaps.

The Xmetryx Feedback Tool *

Closing experience-expectation gaps begins with measuring and understanding them. It is the relationship between expectation (the circumstances that form a baseline *psychological contract*) and experience (the contextual and psychological factors that determine need satisfaction and meaningfulness), that predict the strength and direction of key relationships.

---

* *Patent Pending*

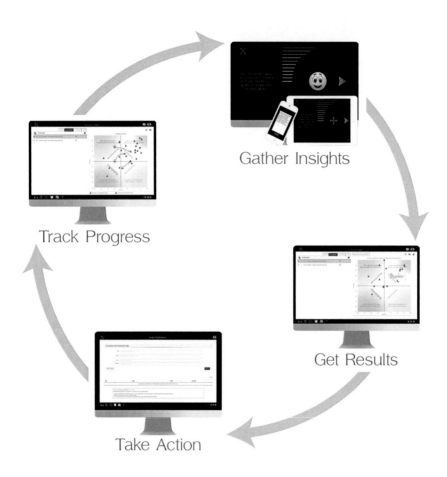

Track Progress

Gather Insights

Get Results

Take Action

Gather insights, get results, take action, and track your progress. Read more about Xmetryx at:

www.xmetryx.com

The Xmetryx feedback tool measures the gaps between what team members expect from their key work relationships and what they are actually experiencing. As it has only three questions, and takes less than three minutes to complete, you can use the Xmetryx feedback tool to gather insights from your teams—local or virtual—on a regular basis, without cutting into already overloaded work days. It's fast and engaging, and delivers powerful insights based upon both affective (feeling) and cognitive (thinking) inputs. The Xmetryx feedback tool combines a consumer look and feel with behavioral science research, making it easy to gather actionable insights and your team members can provide feedback on any device — desktop, tablet, or mobile.

Xmetryx measures the experience of each team member using a graphical sliding scale, in which the expression of an emoticon changes in direct relation to the strength of the positive or negative response. The expectation of the team member is measured next, also using a graphical sliding scale in which a symbol (plus or minus) changes size and color in direct relation to the strength of the response. Terms at the top and bottom of the scale provide additional guidance. Read more about the *Science Behind the Xmetryx Feedback Tool* in the Glossary.

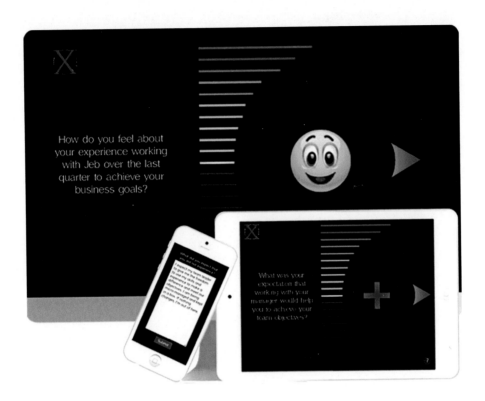

See the Xmetryx feedback tool in action:
www.xmetryx.com/demo

The key to robust feedback is not the number of questions you ask, but what you ask (consider the power of the single Net Promoter™ question for customer experience). The Xmetryx questions have been carefully constructed to elicit rich, candid feedback without bias.

Within Xmetryx, you are able change the subject, target, and time frame — all within in the context of an employee's experience with team leaders, managers, and coworkers. The Xmetryx question format is designed to do three things:

- Get at the heart of each employee's experience by focusing on what is most important to them in key relationships with direct managers, coworkers, and other teams.

- Maintain consistency in questioning for comparison over time.

- Prevent the introduction of bias, to ensure that you're getting accurate data on which you can act.

The Xmetryx feedback tool provides flexibility while maintaining quality and consistency. Keep in mind that, while it is not a general survey tool, with Xmetryx you can customize:

- Subject. An employee's experience with their team members and colleagues on other teams across the organization is as important as their experience with their leader.

- Goal. While Xmetryx covers most outcomes related to team performance, such as business goals and sales targets, your goals might be different. For example, if you're the leader of a development team, maybe you're looking to see how they felt about working with another team on the last sprint. By selecting "Custom Topic" from the topic list, you can choose the wording that works best for your team.

- Time Frame. You can choose to ask about the previous week, month, quarter, or year, or you can choose 'Custom' to define your own time frame (e.g. two-weeks, six-months, etc.).

The Xmetryx Experience Map

As we mentioned earlier, it is our experiences versus our expectations (in the context of key relationships) that affect the direction of our relationships: engaging or disengaging; developing or deteriorating. The Xmetryx Experience Map plots each team member's experience in relation to their expectations as captured by the Xmetryx Feedback Tool. This provides you with a rich picture of any experience-expectation gaps, along with candid feedback that will help guide you in closing those gaps.

The Experience Map is divided into four quadrants which indicate the direction the relationship is headed (counter clockwise from top-right): Engaging, Deteriorating, Disengaging, and Developing.

Xmetryx Experience Gap Score

Along with each Experience Map, Xmetryx provides an Experience Gap Score—the average difference between all your team members' experiences and expectations for a given survey. Ultimately, you want your team responses in the Engaging Quadrant along with a score close to zero (0).

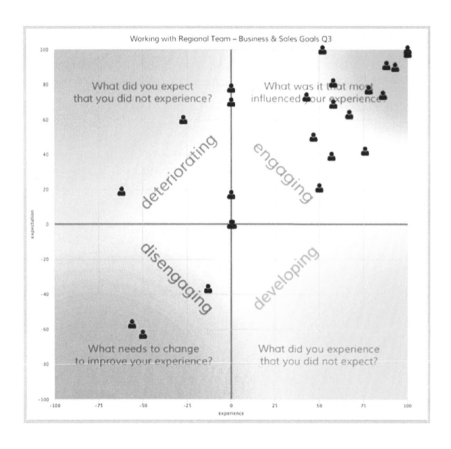

The Engaging Quadrant

This is your *target quadrant*. It indicates team members who have consistently good experiences with high expectations. Team members in this quadrant are likely to have a shared sense of purpose, clear goals, and feel that there are healthy relationships among the team, with coworkers, and with the team leader. You are building trust, loyalty, and confidence that will fuel ongoing team energy, engagement, and performance.

Actions to Take

You are on the path of exceptional team leadership. Continue to reinforce the fundamentals of highly-effective teams, paying particular attention to clear team purpose and supportive team norms. Driving your Experience Gap Score towards zero requires regular communications (weekly, monthly, quarterly), and continuously closing experience-expectation gaps.

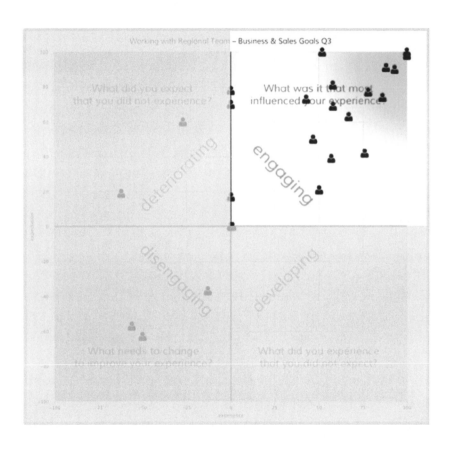

The Deteriorating Quadrant

This is a *transition quadrant* and indicates team members with Negative Experiences and High Expectations. These employees, at one time, had good experiences, which built their high expectations, but experiences have recently become negative. If these issues are not addressed, they will lead to mistrust, uncertainty, and they will begin a transition to disengagement.

Actions to Take

Review your team fundamentals to identify any weaknesses. Focus on clarity in team purpose and goals, as well as team norms (especially psychological safety). At a team level, review and discuss the Experience Map, asking for team input on needed changes to improve overall experiences. At an individual level, get clarity on each team member's expectations versus their current experience across key relationships. Develop an action plan with owners and timing to close gaps.

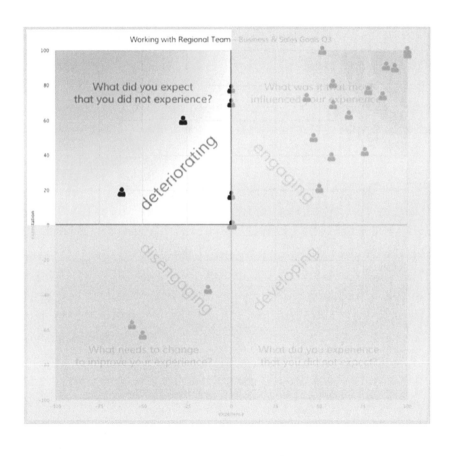

Working with Regional Team — Business & Sales Goals Q3

What did you expect
that you did not experience?

What was it most
influenced our experience

deteriorating

engaging

disengaging

developing

What needs to change
to improve your experience?

What did you experience
that you did not expect?

The Disengaging Quadrant

This is your *crisis quadrant*. Characterized by Negative Experience and Low Expectations, these employees are likely to draw energy away from others on the team, negatively impacting productivity and performance.

Actions to Take

If the majority of the team members fall into this quadrant, then there is likely an issue with the team leader. If the number of people in this quadrant is small, start with 1-on-1 discussions to determine who falls into the Disengaging Quadrant, then assess why expectations are low. Second, identify and prioritize the experiences which will raise expectations. If you do not see rapid improvement, then consider moving the individual(s) to a different team that might offer a better fit.

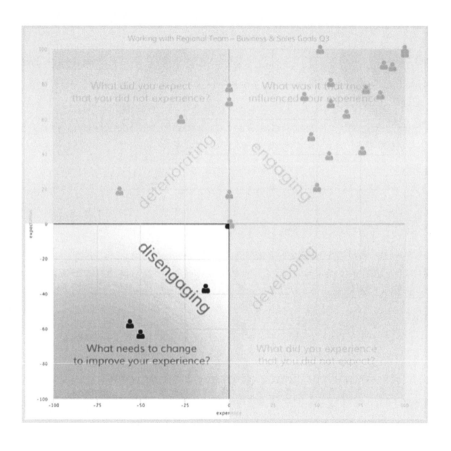

The Developing Quadrant

This is a *transition quadrant* which is characterized by employees with Low to Moderate Expectations and Positive Experiences. These employees are encouraged by their recent experiences, but do not yet have strong trust, loyalty, or confidence, which moderates their expectations.

Actions to Take

Continue to focus on team fundamentals—in particular clarity of purpose and team norms that encourage participation— as well as the key drivers of motivation at work: individual purpose, competence / confidence building through training and knowledge, and increasing autonomy as competencies develop. In addition, ensure that any gaps in experience versus expectations are quickly closed. Your goal is to consistently exceed expectations until they are solidly in the Engaging Quadrant.

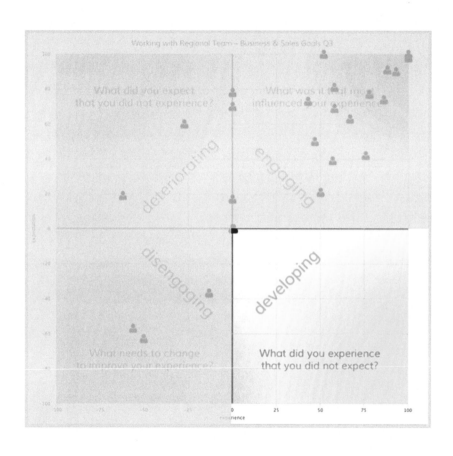

Tracking Progress

We are what we repeatedly do. Developing the one habit of continually closing experience-expectation gaps across key relationships as you build an energized, engaged, and highly-effective team requires discipline and perseverance.

Xmetryx Experience Maps can be combined to track progress as you close these experience-expectation gaps. The ability to set notifications and automated reminders—as well as view the Xmetryx Gap Score Trend, where you can see the change in your team's Experience Gap Score over time—helps you visualize your progress. It also helps you foster the one habit that will move your team into the engaging quadrant.

Within Xmetryx, tracking and Gap Score Trends can be used to compare progress in closing gaps and improving employee experience over time.

Continuous Feedback

Gathering insights on a regular basis—weekly, monthly, and quarterly—is the first step in maintaining key relationships, and requires continuous active participation from your team. It is important to review the Xmetryx feedback tool and method with your team, emphasizing the importance of their candid feedback, and reassuring them that their responses are completely anonymous.

When capturing feedback, focus on key relationships and important goals:

- Team leader / line manager
- Team mates
- Coworkers across functions
- Team Objectives
- Career expectations

Use consistent questions on a recurring basis:

- Weekly or bi-weekly
- Monthly
- Quarterly

Notes: Measuring Gaps

The day the soldiers stop bringing you their problems is the day you stopped leading them. They have either lost confidence that you can help them, or concluded that you do not care. Either case is a failure of leadership.

—*Colin Powell*
Former Chairman of the Joint Chiefs of Staff

Closing Gaps

Across Key
Relationships

The ONE Habit

Closing experience-expectation gaps requires getting to their essence, understanding *what is the gap*, *why is there a gap*, and *how to close the gap*. Just like early-warning radar shows the long-range position and direction of air born threats, the Xmetryx Experience Map reveals the position and direction of the critical relationships that drive energy, engagement, and effectiveness. The gaps identified by Xmetryx, along with candid feedback, provide a starting point for regular discussions.

For teams and team leaders, developing *the one habit of discussing and closing experience-expectation gaps* is central to building trust, engagement, and highly-energized and effective teams. Important actions to develop the one habit include:

- Weekly Individual Check-ins
- Monthly Team Reviews
- Quarterly 1-on-1 Reviews

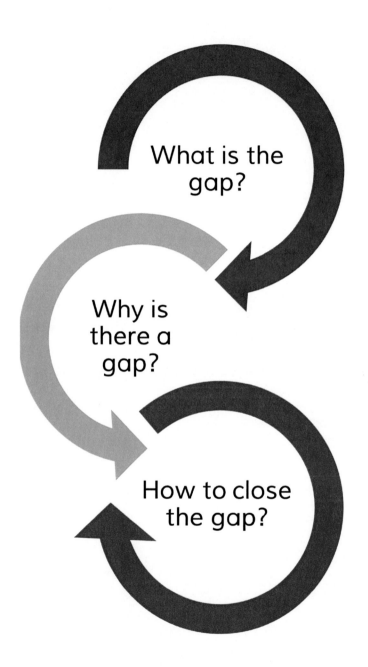

Weekly Individual Check-ins

Taking time each week for a short 1-on-1 check-in with every member of your team is critical to keeping individuals energized. These check-ins are an opportunity to touch base with your team members, keeping them energized and focused on their goals and progress—like a weekly battery recharge.

During these check-ins, your bias should be toward asking questions versus giving direction, and reinforcing support for the individual rather than getting a report.

Make it social, rather than formal—have a chat over coffee or, when circumstances make that impractical, via email or text. The idea is to keep these conversations outside the conference room. Lastly, be sure to mention key experience-expectation gaps and the efforts and / or progress in addressing them.

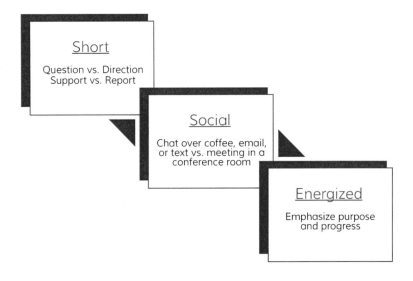

Notes: Weekly Individual Check-ins

_____

_____

_____

_____

_____

_____

_____

_____

_____

_____

_____

_____

_____

_____

_____

_____

_____

_____

Monthly Team Reviews

Monthly Team reviews should focus on your team's performance in relation to progress toward their goals, ensure clarity and alignment on the team's processes and purpose, and review the latest feedback to identify any new experience-expectation gaps.

Exceptional team leaders ensure that their monthly reviews generate actions. Use this time to confirm alignment on team priorities, identify what's needed to close any gaps—assign an owner and set a target date for each action—and verify that the resources needed to achieve the team's goals are available.

During these discussions, review your team's Experience Map and use it to create robust conversations around what is working well, and what needs to be improved within your team and with other teams across the organization. Emphasize the fundamentals of highly-effective teams, especially purpose, goals, and upholding team norms.

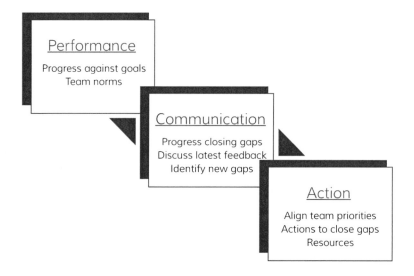

Performance
Progress against goals
Team norms

Communication
Progress closing gaps
Discuss latest feedback
Identify new gaps

Action
Align team priorities
Actions to close gaps
Resources

Notes: Monthly Team Reviews

_____

_____

_____

_____

_____

_____

_____

_____

_____

_____

_____

_____

_____

_____

_____

_____

_____

_____

_____

Quarterly 1-on-1 Reviews

The quarterly 1-on-1 review gives you time for a more formal discussion of each team member's performance over the previous quarter, as well as an opportunity to set both short term and longer term goals for the next three months to one year. These discussions should focus on your team member's individual performance in relation to their personal and team goals. Also, be sure to touch on how they're holding to the established team norms. For example, are they encouraging conversation equality among team members? Do they feel secure in taking risks and sharing ideas?

Finally, it is important that your team member's career and purpose is a central focus of these discussions, not just the goals of the team. Review their support needs, discussing what they require in the way of resources, information, and training to be successful. Be sure you understand their career expectations, what progress they have made toward their personal goals, and how you, as a team leader, can support their growth.

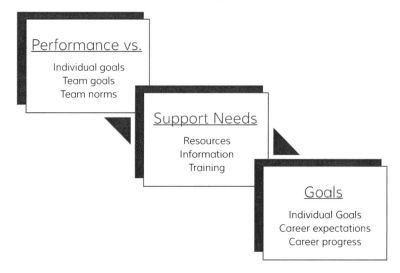

Performance vs.
Individual goals
Team goals
Team norms

Support Needs
Resources
Information
Training

Goals
Individual Goals
Career expectations
Career progress

Notes: Quarterly 1-on-1 Reviews

_____

_____

_____

_____

_____

_____

_____

_____

_____

_____

_____

_____

_____

_____

_____

_____

_____

Exceptional Results

The gaps identified by Xmetryx provide a starting point for regular discussions. For teams and team leaders, developing the one habit of discussing and closing experience-expectation gaps is central to building trust, engagement, and highly-energized and effective teams.

Use Xmetryx to identify the gaps in key relationships that can inhibit team energy and effectiveness. Then use the tools within Xmetryx — such as Conversation Reminders, Action Reminders, and Tracking — to continue to develop the one habit that leads to lasting change, team excellence, and exceptional results.

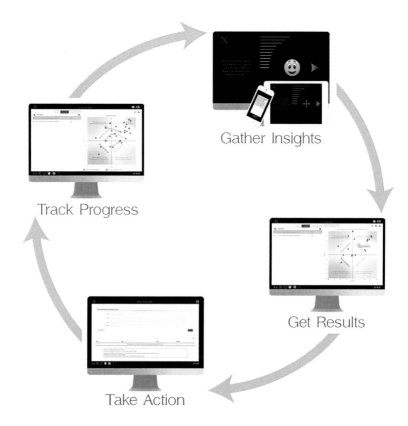

Gather Insights

Track Progress

Get Results

Take Action

Notes: Experience-Expectation Gaps

Perfection is not attainable, but
if we chase perfection we can
catch excellence.

—*Vince Lombardi*
Former Head Coach, Green Bay Packers

Getting Started

Building
the Best Team

Building the Best Team

Teams are shaping the future of work and organizations. Building a highly-effective team that is energized and fully engaged is a blend of art and science. The essence of that alchemy is the three elements that make up the Architecture of Highly-Effective Teams:

1. Team Fundamentals: Ensure that the essential building blocks of a highly-effective team architecture are in place: *Purpose*, *People*, and *Support*. There are no short-cuts to getting these fundamentals right. It takes discipline, patience, and perseverance.

2. Individual Motivation: Ensure you get the most out of your foundation of solid team fundamentals by *applying a working knowledge of motivation at work*. Meeting your team's core psychological needs drives energy, engagement, and performance.

3. Key Relationships: Gaps between our experiences and our expectations affect energy, motivation, and engagement. By using Xmetryx on a regular basis to measure and understand experience-expectation gaps, you can *focus on the one habit of closing those gaps across key relationships*.

At the beginning of this Guide we said that it is first and foremost a means to an end. Follow the steps in this Guide to implement the Architecture of Highly-Effective Teams. It will help you focus on the actions that build solid team fundamentals, motivate people at work, and develop the habit of closing experience-expectation gaps across key relationships.

From experience, we know that busy team leaders need tools and methods that are easy to use and fit naturally into already overloaded work days. Xmetryx was designed by team leaders for team leaders, to develop the *ONE Habit* that leads to energized, engaged, highly-effective teams.

Getting Started Checklist

Whether you have inherited a long-standing team, or are creating a new team, use the check-list below to ensure that you have put the Architecture of Highly-Effective Teams in place.

Team Fundamentals

☐ Clear purpose and goals

☐ The people

    ☐ Healthy team norms

    ☐ Clear job design

    ☐ Optimal team size

☐ Optimal level of team support

    ☐ Resources

    ☐ Information

    ☐ Training

Motivation at Work

☐ Individuals have a clear purpose

    ☐ Individuals have the autonomy (freedom) to do their work

    ☐ Continuous investment in competence and confidence

Key Relationships

    ☐ Measure and understand experience vs expectation

    ☐ Develop the one habit of closing experience-expectation gaps

    ☐ Conduct regular conversations and track progress

Notes: Getting Started

Teams are the core of organizational success, and the experiences of the people on those teams are at the heart of team success.

—*Jeb Hurley*
Author, The ONE Habit

Our Story

Over the course of our collective 50 years of experience, we have worked within both mature multinational corporations and leading-edge tech start-ups. We have had the privilege of being part of high performance teams, and have suffered the pain of being on teams that were highly-dysfunctional. We have sat through countless training and development presentations, courses, and workshops where many powerful ideas were presented. Very few created new habits and lasting results.

Our experiences forged the belief that teams are the future of work and organizations, and led to research on team motivation, engagement, and performance. The results of this research revealed the tremendous impact that a team's architecture, and the health of key relationships, have on team energy and effectiveness.

The Architecture of Highly-Effective Teams, the ONE Habit of exceptional team leaders, and the Xmetryx tools emerged from those experiences and research. Our purpose is to enable organizations to cost-effectively build energized, highly-effective teams. In doing so, we help leaders elevate the employee experience, creating positive energy that benefits the well-being of the people, their organization, and the communities in which they live.

Dr. Jeb S. Hurley, DBA
Author and Xmetryx Co-founder

Jeb's passion for building businesses was fueled by early experiences working in his family's business, being part of the team that took a fast growing tech start-up into Europe, and launching a new product category for a Japanese company. One path on his career journey led Jeb to global business unit VP / GM roles at two multi-nationals. A second path led him to CEO roles at a VC-backed imaging technology start-up and an established software company, and the cofounding of two software businesses. More recently, the two paths converged as Jeb has led multiple projects and teams at HP Inc. in the Asia-Pacific region, and co-founded Xmetryx, a software company that is creating cloud-based tools to help organizations build more effective teams and exceptional team leaders.

Jeb complemented his 25-plus years of global, cross-cultural leadership experience with leadership programs at the Center for Creative Leadership, The Aspen Institute, and Harvard Business School. Most recently, Jeb earned a doctorate in leadership with a focus on motivation, engagement, and team performance.

http://linkedin.com/in/jebhurley

Elena A. Newton
Editor and Xmetryx Co-founder

Elena began her career as employee number 16 at a software startup, with responsibilities ranging from technical writing to operations. After the company was acquired by a Dutch multinational, she held various leadership roles focusing on both customer and technical areas of the business. Ultimately, she lead the establishment of their Global Services organization, with responsibility for all aspects of the experience of the company's +10,000 customers. In addition, Elena took on the design and development overhaul of a failing product, building it into a consumer friendly, subscription based offering. Elena went on to co-found a customer experience technology startup, providing customer experience and consulting services to a broad range of global clients, before she pivoted her career to focus on her passion for software design and development.

Elena's blend of product design and development talent, and her unrelenting focus on execution excellence, enables her to manage all aspects of the Xmetryx experience, from coding and design, to customer relationships and publishing.

https://linkedin.com/in/ea0723

Resources

Example: Sales Team Goal Setting

Organization Goals

- *Total revenue growth* _____
- *Improved gross margin* _____
- _____
- _____
- _____

Team Goals

- *Unit sales into specific target market segments* _____
- *Revenue growth at higher average selling price* _____
- _____
- _____
- _____
- _____

Performance Measures

1. *Change in margin % by customer* _____
2. *Sales to existing customers* _____
3. *Total customer experience* _____
4. _____
5. _____
6. _____

Team Goal Setting Template

Organization Goals

- _____
- _____
- _____
- _____
- _____

Team Goals

- _____
- _____
- _____
- _____
- _____
- _____

Performance Measures

1. _____
2. _____
3. _____
4. _____
5. _____
6. _____

Example: Relationship Mapping

Example Reporting Structure

	CEO	
VP of Sales		VP of Engineering
James		Roger
Alex Emily		Ilya Andrew
Quinn Val		Cathy

Key Relationships (for Sales Team)

- *Product Development*

- *Marketing*

- *Service*

Formal Communications (by Sales Team)

- *Monthly status report to VP of Engineering*

- *Weekly stand-up with Service*

- *Quarterly market review, Marketing & Product*

Informal Communications (by Sales Team)

1. *Emily -> Ilya, weekly check-ins*

2. *Quinn -> Roger ,*

3. *Andrew -> James bi-weekly coffee*

4.

Relationship Mapping Template

Key Relationships

- _____
- _____
- _____
- _____
- _____

Formal Communications

- _____
- _____
- _____
- _____
- _____
- _____

Informal Communications

- _____
- _____
- _____
- _____
- _____
- _____

Example: Defining Team Context

Team Context

- *Global Virtual Team*

- *Three countries (US, Spain, Singapore)*
- *Six people, five cultures*
- *Up to 15-hours time difference*
- *No direct reporting relationships*
-
-
-
-
-
-
-
-
-
-
-
-
-
-

Team Context Template

Team Context

- _____

- _____

- _____

- _____

- _____

- _____

- _____

- _____

- _____

- _____

- _____

- _____

- _____

- _____

- _____

- _____

- _____

- _____

Example: Team Competency Needs

Needs

- _Technical product knowledge_ _____

- _Local language_ _____

- _Financial understanding_ _____

- _Relationship management_ _____

- _____

- _____

- _____

- _____

- _____

Gaps / Areas to Strengthen

- _New product training_ _____

- _Financial analysis_ _____

- _____

- _____

- _____

- _____

- _____

- _____

- _____

Team Competency Needs Template

Needs

- _____
- _____
- _____
- _____
- _____
- _____
- _____
- _____
- _____

Gaps / Areas to Strengthen

- _____
- _____
- _____
- _____
- _____
- _____
- _____
- _____
- _____

Example: Team Resource Needs

Goal / Objective (from Team Goals template)

- *Unit sales into specific target market segments*

- *Revenue growth at higher average selling price*

- _____

- _____

- _____

Need / Resource Gaps

1. *Understand the market / Competitive landscape*

2. *Reduce discounts / Reduce service requirements*

3. _____

4. _____

5. _____

6.

Owner / Target Date

1. *Val / End of Q1*

2. *Alex / mid-Q1*

3. _____

4. _____

5. _____

6. _____

Team Resource Needs Template

Goals / Objectives

- _____
- _____
- _____
- _____
- _____

Need / Resource Gaps

1. _____
2. _____
3. _____
4. _____
5. _____
6.

Owner / Target Date

1. _____
2. _____
3. _____
4. _____
5. _____
6. _____

Example: Team Information Needs

Goal / Objective (from Team Goals template)

* _Unit sales into specific target market segments_

* _Revenue growth at higher average selling price_

* _____

* _____

* _____

Information Needs / Sources

1. _Quarterly Competitive Landscape / Marketing_

2. _Regular Updates on Product Issues / Service_

3. _____

4. _____

5. _____

6.

Owner

1. _Emily - Marketing, quarterly_

2. _Quinn - Account Service Managers, weekly_

3. _____

4. _____

5. _____

6. _____

Team Information Needs Template

Goals / Objectives

- _____

- _____

- _____

- _____

- _____

Information Needs / Sources

1. _____

2. _____

3. _____

4. _____

5. _____

6.

Owner

1. _____

2. _____

3. _____

4. _____

5. _____

6. _____

Additional Reading

Battistelli, A., Galletta, M., Portoghese, I., & Vandenberghe, C. (2013). Mindsets of commitment and motivation: Interrelationships and contribution to work outcomes. *The Journal of Psychology*, 147, 17–48. doi:10.1080/00223980.2012.668146

Beer, M., Finnström, M., Schrader, D. (October, 2016). Why leadership training fails - and what to do about it. *Harvard Business Review*, 10, 50–57. https://hbr.org/2016/10/why-leadership-training-fails-and-what-to-do-about-it

Deci, E. L., & Ryan, R. M. (1985). Intrinsic motivation and self-determination in human behavior. New York, NY: Plenum

Deci, E. L., & Ryan, R. M. (2012). Motivation, personality, and development within embedded social contexts: An overview of self-determination theory. In R. M. Ryan (Ed.), *The Oxford Handbook of Human Motivation*, (pp. 85–107). New York, NY: Oxford University Press.

Gagné, M., & Deci, E. L. (2005). Self-determination theory and work motivation. *Journal of Organizational Behavior*, 26, 331–362. doi:10.1002/job.322

Kahn, W. A. (1990). Psychological conditions of personal engagement and disengagement at work. *Academy of Management Journal*, 33, 692–724. doi:10.2307/256287

LaTour, S. A., and Peat, N. C. (1979), Conceptual and Methodological Issues in Consumer Satisfaction Research, in *Advances in Consumer Research*, (Vol. 6), ed. William L. Wilkie, *Ann Arbor: Association for Consumer Research*, 431–440.

Oliver, R. L. (1977). Effect of expectation and disconfirmation on post-exposure product evaluations: An alternative interpretation. *Journal of Applied Psychology*, 62(4), 480–486. doi:10.1037/0021-9010.62.4.480

Oliver R. L. (1980). A Cognitive Model of the Antecedents and Consequences of Satisfaction Decisions, *Journal of Marketing Research*, 17(4), p. 460. doi:10.2307/3150499

Olson, J. C., & Dover, P. (1976). Effects of Expectation Creation and Disconfirmation on Belief Elements of Cognitive Structure, in B. B. Anderson, ed., *Advances in Consumer Research*, Volume III, Chicago: *Association for Consumer Research*, 168–175.

Rousseau, D. M. (1989). Psychological and implied contracts in organizations. *Employee Responsibilities and Rights Journal*, 2(2), 121–139.

Ryan, R. M., & Deci, E. L. (2000). Self-determination theory and the facilitation of intrinsic motivation, social development, and well-being. *American Psychologist*, 55, 68–78. doi:10.1037/0003-066X.55.1.68

Schaufeli, W. B. (2013). What is engagement? In C. Truss, K. Alfes, R. Delbridge, A. Shantz, and E.C. Soane (Eds.), *Employee Engagement in Theory and Practice*, (pp. 1–38) London: Routledge.

Truss, C., Shantz, A., Soane, E., Alfes, K., & Delbridge, R. (2013). Employee engagement, organisational performance and individual well-being: Exploring the evidence, developing the theory. *International Journal of Human Resource Management*, 24, 2657–2669. doi:10.1080/09585192.2013.798921

Glossary

Autonomy

Identified within Self-determination Theory (SDT) as one of three universal psychological needs that drives human motivation, Autonomy is the need to have control over one's own role and priorities.

See Self-Determination Theory

Competence

One of three universal psychological needs identified within SDT that drives human motivation, Competence is the need to develop and demonstrate one's capabilities and capacities.

See Self-Determination Theory

Engagement Theory

At the intersection of employee well-being and performance lies the concept of engagement. Over the past 25 years, engagement has become a ubiquitous construct within business. In his seminal research on personal engagement and disengagement at work, Kahn (1990) introduced the engagement framework which describes how work experience and work context inform personal engagement and task performance.

Kahn, W. A. (1990). Psychological conditions of personal engagement and disengagement at work. *Academy of Management Journal, 33*, 692–724. doi:10.2307/256287

Expectancy Disconfirmation Theory

As noted by R. L. Oliver (1977 and 1980), expectancy disconfirmation theory (alternatively expectation disconfirmation theory, expectation confirmation theory, ECT) is a cognitive theory which seeks to explain the impact of expectations, and confirmation / disconfirmation of (experience with) those expectations.

Oliver R. L, (1977), "Effect of Expectation and Disconfirmation on Postexposure Product Evaluations - an Alternative Interpretation," *Journal of Applied Psychology*, 62(4), p. 480.

Oliver R. L, (1980). A Cognitive Model of the Antecedents and Consequences of Satisfaction Decisions, *Journal of Marketing Research*, 17(4), p. 460.

Expectations

Expectations can be defined as an individual's belief about the experience he or she will have in a given scenario. Expectations can be the result of past experience with similar situations, or knowledge about other peoples' experiences with similar situations.

Olson, J. C., & Dover, P. (1976). Effects of Expectation Creation and Disconfirmation on Belief Elements of Cognitive Structure, in B. B. Anderson, ed., Advances in Consumer Research, Volume III, Chicago: *Association for Consumer Research*, 168–75.

LaTour, S. A., Peat, N. C. (1979). Conceptual and Methodological Issues in Consumer Satisfaction Research, in Advances in Consumer Research, (Vol. 6), ed. William L. Wilkie, Ann Arbor: *Association for Consumer Research*, 431–440.

Job Design

Job design is the process of putting together a range of tasks, duties, and responsibilities to create a composite for individuals to undertake in their work and to regard as their own.

> Torrington et al., 2011. *Human Resource Management*. 8th Edition. Harlow: Pearson.

Key Relationships

Key work relationships are those relationships that have a high degree of impact on goal achievement, career advancement, and role satisfaction. They are characterized by a high degree of both emotional (affective) and cognitive engagement. Consider not just the job itself, but also the way the team member is intended to interact with those around them.

The primary key relationships, as mentioned in this guide, are:

- The relationship between a team member and his or her team leader.
- The relationship between a team member and another person on the same team.
- The relationship between a team member and people on other teams).

Psychological Contract Theory

A psychological contract, a concept developed in contemporary research by organizational scholar Denise Rousseau, represents the mutual beliefs, perceptions, and informal obligations between an employer and an employee. It sets the dynamics for the relationship and defines the detailed practicality of the work to be done.

> Rousseau, D. M. (1989). Psychological and implied contracts in organizations. *Employee Responsibilities and Rights Journal,* 2: 121–139. https://www.wikiwand.com/en/Psychological_contract

Purpose

One of three universal psychological needs that drives human motivation, Purpose is the sense of belonging and believing that one's work makes a difference.

See Self-Determination Theory

Role Content

Designed to enable people to find their work meaningful, and to help them feel that the work they do matters and makes a difference. Role content should:

- Foster a sense of responsibility, and allow people to see the link between the work they do and the end results of their work.

- Allow people to use their current skills and develop new ones.

- See how their work contributes to a 'whole piece' of work.

- Have a sense of autonomy.

- Receive regular and constructive feedback.

Role Context

Role context comprises the reality of the organizational culture, the team norms, everyday work processes, the nature of key relationships and dependencies, as well as key measures of success. It also frames the conditions under which work is performed and the demands such work imposes on employees. Good role context should clearly identify:

- Reporting relationships
- Supervision received
- Judgment, authority
- Personal contacts (key relationships)
- Physical and mental demands

Science Behind the Xmetryx Feedback Tool

Xmetryx measures the experience of each team member on a –100 to +100 scale using a bipolar, graphic-based visual analog scale (dynamic emoticon and color). The baseline expectation of each team member is measured via a continuous interval scale with semantic differentiation (–100 to +100), represented on a sliding scale using visual and color cues.

Traditional scales (such as 5 to 10-point integer scales) can result in data skewing or overall mean scores that are less accurate.

Learn more about the Xmetryx feedback tool online: www.xmetryx.com.

Self-Determination Theory

Self-Determination Theory (SDT) is a theory of motivation. It is concerned with supporting our natural—or intrinsic—tendencies to behave in effective and healthy ways. SDT has been researched and practiced by a network of researchers around the world. www.selfdeterminationtheory.org

> Deci, E. L., & Ryan, R. M. (1985). *Intrinsic Motivation and Self-determination in Human Behavior*. New York, NY: Plenum

Team Norms

The traditions, behavioral standards, and unwritten rules of a group. For example:

- The methods team members use interact and communicate with each other.
- The methods team members use to communicate with members of other teams.
- The methods team members use to take responsibility and accountability for accomplishing their group goals.

Index

A

B

C

D

E

K

Key relationships 4, 7, 12, 28, 34, 35, 42, 46, 48, 52, 60, 72, 76, 82, 102, 104

Knowledge 34, 56, 76, 101

L

Leader performance 42

Leadership 3, 50, 82, 83, 84, 96

Loyalty 50, 56

M

Meaningfulness 42

Monthly 50, 60, 68

Motivation 4, 6, 7, 24, 28, 29, 37, 56, 76, 96, 97, 100, 103, 105

Motivational drive theories 29

  Behavioral 29

  Psychodynamic 29

N

Need satisfaction 42

P

People 19, 25, 76

Positive energy 25

Psychological Contract Theory 35, 103

Psychological needs 25, 76, 100, 103

Psychological safety 14, 52

Psychologies

  Applied 29

  Experimental 29

Psychology 25

Purpose 12, 19, 27, 76, 103

Q

Quadrant 48, 50, 52, 54, 56
Quarterly 50, 60, 70

R

Resources 7, 16, 18, 78
Results 25, 26, 42, 72, 78, 103
Richard Ryan 29
Role 25, 29, 84, 100, 102, 104
Ryan, Richard 29

S

Satisfying 25
Self-Determination Theory 29, 35
Skill mastery 25
Skills 17, 34, 103
Social intelligence 14
Subconscious 24
Support 76

T

Target quadrant 50
Team architecture 19, 76
Team effectiveness 42
Team fundamentals 4, 6, 10, 52, 56, 76
Team performance 42
The one habit 6, 64, 72, 76, 78, 82
Thinking 43, 46
Training 17, 18, 78
Transition quadrant 52, 56
Trust 50, 56, 64, 72

W
Weekly 60, 66, 88

X
Xmetryx 6, 42–62, 43, 45–48, 58–60, 64, 72, 76, 82–84, 104

Notes

experience • expectation • excellence

Learn more about Xmetryx on our website:

www.xmetryx.com

Made in the USA
San Bernardino, CA
21 February 2019